AF449499

Eyes These

APAALA RAJ NEGI

BlueRose ONE
Stories Matter

© Apaala Raj Negi 2023

All rights reserved

All rights reserved by author. No part of this publication may be reproduced, stored in a retrieval system or transmitted in any form or by any means, electronic, mechanical, photocopying, recording or otherwise, without the prior permission of the author.

Although every precaution has been taken to verify the accuracy of the information contained herein, the author and publisher assume no responsibility for any errors or omissions. No liability is assumed for damages that may result from the use of information contained within.

First Published in March 2023

ISBN: 978-93-5741-277-3

BLUEROSE PUBLISHERS

www.BlueRoseONE.com

info@bluerosepublishers.com

+91 8882 898 898

Cover Design:

Muskan Sachdeva

Typographic Design:

Rohit

Distributed by: BlueRose, Amazon, Flipkart

To the readers,

That's eventually you; whom I wrote this
book for.

Contents

Chapter-1

HOME

The melody of a lullaby crawled around the veils of a bed. It wasn't being sung by someone now, it didn't feel original enough. And kept buzzing in her sleep, she was too deep in sleep for a chirm noise to wake her up. The noise was now getting in her vicinity but not disturbing enough to startle her from her sweet deep sleep.

She didn't notice it until a soft cloth got hard around her neck……hard until she couldn't breathe and it became the bind of death….

The bind wasn't strong enough to break her neck, there was a gentle touch in the hands of the murderer, but the bind was still strong enough to suffocate her to death.

All she could do now was to wait for her murderer to finish the task. Fighting or struggling was out of her level. All she could do was choke and move her limbs. The struggle continued and a locket fell from the murderer's neck, that was all she could see as her vision started to get blurry.

But then a force grabbed the hands away and she took the breath of life.

Now all she could hear were screams and not lullaby.

"You, okay?" a women asked from the driving seat to the girl who just sat next to her on the passenger seat and closed the door. she handed over a bottle of water.

"Yeah…… just…." Savanna replied as she accepted the bottle and rubbed her temples simultaneously.

"The nightmares again….huh….?" Her mother asked turning the key.

"Hmmm….."

The nightmares haunted her from as earlier as she could remember. She didn't know, why or how, but they were now a part of her life routine.

She lived her whole life with her divorced mother and never met her father, because her mother always excused to be busy in her business and Savanna didn't even mind it, for her a person out of sight was a person out of mind. There was no contact between her and her father, no connections, hence, no emotions and that's why it didn't even hurt her much when the news of her father's demise was announced by her mother. It was more of a sudden news than a sad news for her. And now that her father was no more her grandmother was left all alone, and they were shifting to her house to take care of her.

Her home was a traditional wooden house, renovated but so old, it made her truly believe that at least one or two ghosts might be dawdling in the corridors. The front yard was denser than she had ever expected a garden with a caretaker to be, it was as if the caretaker didn't even want the unwanted weeds to lay life less on the ground, and now the ground was home to trees, plants, flowers and, weed.

The stone steps led to an open Mahogany door, inside was an old woman in the living room, relaxing on a velvet sofa in front of the fireplace and wearing the granny glasses chain, she was staring into the nothingness in the fire.

"Hey mom, it's me, Sharon" Her mother said it in such a tone to the back of the sofa, that it made her doubt if her grandmother was suffering from Alzheimer or something.

She stood up more slowly than a sloth would, adjusting her glasses and staring at Savanna, when Sharin hugged her.

"You've grown so much" granny said to her.

"Grown?"

"Yes... grown old"

"But your sense of humor doesn't look like to be getting old." Sharin laughed it off.

"Oh..., I've already grown old enough to never age in my life, and now let me talk to your daughter." All of a sudden, a boost of energy hit her, she kind of ran to Savanna, stared at her as if trying to read a board without glasses. She then traced her dark circle under her glasses as if to hide her tears and said...

"These eyes..."

She wondered whether she said it to herself or to Savanna, as this was a comment she usually used to receive. Grandmother gave her a tight hug, which felt nothing like a hug, maybe because she felt nothing like love from her ever before and that may be because it was the first time, she was talking to her in ten years.

Sitting on her grandmother's sofa in front of the fireplace and writing in her journal was quite comfortable, even if it was hot summer outside.

"You write diary entries?" grandmother asked as she entered the living room in the evening.

"Yes, since I was twelve."

"Same"

"Since you were twelve?"

"No, but I write"

She sat down on the sofa next to the other one, staring the nothingness into the fire of summer.

"Did you miss me? all these years...?"

She asked promptly, still staring the fire.

"Yes..." She hesitated and lied.

Grandmother nodded but said nothing. Seconds passed by when she said.

"Now I will ask you something and this time my dear tell me the truth." For the first time moving her eyes from the fire to her.

Savanna nodded.

"Does this home feel like home to you?"

This question didn't make any sense to her, so she stayed blank trying to understand the thing again.

She waited for the answer, but when there was no response she said, "Mmmmm... I can understand, sometimes home doesn't feel like home." With this she slowly stood up and started walking towards the stairs.

"At least there is one thing passed on to her through generations."

Savanna heard the grandmother murmuring to herself.

Chapter-2

PHOTOFRAMES

"Was sir Regin really your father?" a random kid at her new school asked.

She only nodded, feeling reluctant to answer as this was the twelfth time, she heard this question being asked from her, and hating the way he emphasized on the word 'your'.

"And you never saw him."

"I –kind of did"

"How….? tell us everything" another random kid asked.

"Well, my parents got divorced, when I was 6, since then I never saw him."

"Your parents didn't go well together? Right?

"Don't you think you are being way too personal?"

Her father was the principal in the school she was studying right now and every student there was way too interested in learning about his 'mysterious life.'

The more anyone asked about her father the more she realized her ignorance towards him. The only option she tripped on to get rid of these awkward questions was to ignore all of them and join her history class twenty minutes earlier. Just when she was about to touch the door knob, someone opens and slams the door hard on her face, and she tumbles on the floor, holding her nose, pretty sure that it was going to bleed.

"Hey, you okay....? I am sorry, I was just in a hurry." She heard someone say this while sitting on the floor next to her. She was in enough pain to not open her eyes for the next hour, all she did was hear him collecting the books she accidently threw and placing it next to her knees. She felt like he stared her for a second and then left shouting "I am still in a hurry by the way, sorry once again, Miss Husky."

And now she was late for her class, as she had to make sure her nose wasn't bleeding anymore and when she opened the same door to enter the class, everyone stared at her as if she had just proposed the theory of having two livers.

"Please come and introduce yourself Miss late comer." A short man wearing a long coat said this in the most sarcastic way possible. She slowly walked to the lecture podium and introduced herself only to the prof. in a whispering tone.

"I am Savanna Smith."

The lines of anger between his brows turned into the lines of surprise. And he looked at her as if her theory of two livers turned out to be right.

"Are you Regin's daughter?" He whispered back to her while the class stared them in confusion.

She nodded.

He nodded back and gestured her to take a seat.

"What was he whispering to you?" the boy sitting next to her asked.

"The same question everyone does." She replied and flicked through the pages of her book.

"Whether you are professor Regin's daughter or not. Right?"

"How do you know?"

"My parents knew him and I've seen a photograph from an album at my parent's home, Professor Regin and you, you were five years old though, and there is no doubt of news flowing in the school about Prof's daughter's admission."

"And how did you know that it is me?

He took a pause from scribbling in the notebook and pointed with his pen to her eyes.

"These eyes" he said.

The awkward silence continued until he introduced himself.

"I am Joe, by the way"

"And I am Samantha" someone said from the backseat leaning over to Savanna.

"Joe's best friend" she added.'

"No, she is not" he replied.

"Anyway, have you caught up with the syllabus??" she asked.

"I shifted here not more than a week ago. Moreover, this is my first day in this High School."

"Brilliant, Joe can help you with that. He LOVES to do that."

"Well, that I would like to do."

"Great then." Samantha clapped her hands.

"We'll see you at your house today then. And kindly tell us your address because I don't think anyone knows where Regin the Dracula lived."

"SAMANTHA. Shut up" Joe whispered.

"Woah....! Your mum is way too friendly to be vamp..." Sam stopped and changed her words mid-sentence when she saw Joe staring at her and continued.

"I mean …to be Professor Regin's wife"

"Was he that rude?" Savanna asked

Her mother was way too happy to find Savanna talking to people because all She did do in her life was hibernating in her room for 367 days of the year.

"He wasn't rude actually, he was just quiet, and people generally mistake it to being rude." Joe said instead of Samantha.

"I'll have to admit though, I am disappointed." Samantha said staring at the ceiling.

No one asked why and she explained herself.

"Because I expected your home to be a long tower or a cave or…"

"Wait…. wait a minute. How do you even come up with these baseless theories?" Joe asked.

"Heyy, everyone thinks students have collected evidence of him being a vampire." She argued.

"Well then Savanna, I want you to turn this girl into a vampire, so that she wakes up only in the night and doesn't irritate me during the days."

"That wasn't funny." Samantha said back.

"And if you can try and change her hairs with your powers, it would be your great kindness."

Samantha had super curly and messy hair. She was chubby as well as buck teethed giving her a look of a wild rabbit.

"Anyways, are these your family photographs above the stairs? Samantha asked pointing to the staircase around the fireplace.

"Hmm..." that was all she replied tired of hearing their baseless argument.

Samantha and Joe walked to the staircase followed later by Savanna.

In the first frame, the 5 old savanna was peeking down out of a treehouse built on a banyan tree.

"My father clicked it." Savanna said.

"You remember that...?"

"I.....don't remember anything to all these photos. My grandmother told me all about this."

In the next frame, Regin Smith was acting as a dead pirate while Savanna sat on a treasure chest smiling over her victory, wearing the pirate eye cover, and that signature smile on her face.

"Professor looks happy" Joe said in utter surprise.

"Isn't that normal?" Savanna asked surprisingly to see both surprised.

"No, I swear, I've never saw him smiling in my whole life" Joe said.

And the next frame was her parents photograph and an infant Savanna in her mother's arms.

"Granny says, it's the only photograph we have together."

"How is that even possible?" Samantha asked.

"I don't know, may be the others are lost or may we be don't really have any, they were together only for five years after my birth and even those weren't any peaceful years and after divorce, they never met each other."

Chapter-3

FAIRY TALES

* I've been in the Shadows.

The water deep but shallow

But you were there

and everything was beautiful *

Listening to songs in her earphones, and walking under the star, was her favorite thing to do. Eyes closed and cool winds hitting her skin and the noise of circlets and puppies.

"Puppies?" she wondered.

A boy was coming from the opposite side of the road with a puppy, enjoying his night walk to the fullest.

Savanna with no hesitation walked over to the boy and asked,

"Is it your husky?" she asked and bent down to have a better look at the puppy.

"Yup" he replied not trying to remove his hoodie or move his eyes away from his phone.

"Who are you? He asked.

"Savanna Smith"

"Regin's daughter?"

"hmm"

"You are my neighbor then, just three blocks away."

"Do you like dogs by the way? He asked.

"Huskies"

"I see" he sighed.

"This Husky's grandmother disappeared mysteriously. Just a fun fact"

"How did that happen?"

"May be the animal rescue took her or she ran away and decided to become a street dog one day randomly." he laughed.

"Anyway, I should go now. See you soon." He took his husky in his in his arms and walked away. She didn't even see his face as he had his hood up the whole time even when he walked away.

It wasn't more than nine when she walked into her room, removed the earphones, and laid silent on her bed.

She was silent but her room wasn't ....

After a few minutes, she realized the presence of an unwanted music in her room. The music was feeble, she had to focus all her mind on it to make sure she was not hallucinating. And no, she wasn't hallucinating.

"So, you woke up to a nightmare?" Samantha asked leaning towards savanna and joe's seats.

"And you doubt that it was due to that unpleasant music? Joe asked.

"Considering that I had the nightmare just the next morning after I heard that music."

"Told you.... your house is haunted" Samantha snapped.

"Would you mind to keep your volume low; we are in the classroom?" savanna said

"Actually, you told me that my father was a vampire."

"Who knows, he knew dark magic and something of that sort too" Samantha said.

"What kind of connection do you find in dark magic and some music?" Joe asked

"I have other theories too, some of the people in our class told me that...."

"No need, no need. I don't think that's what we are discussing."

"My nightmares." Savanna said.

"Then you will have to go to a psychiatrist." Samantha said and leaned back on her seat.

"Oh...wait! I have a better option." She said just a second later.

"What!" Savanna asked.

"I know a person, who might have the same experience as you."

"Go on!" Joe said.

"Ok... ok... so, I have heard that he used to get nightmares way often, maybe he can help you in some way."

"Sam ... No." Joe said.

"Yes." Sam said.

"That's the only way out." She continued.

"What?? You guys gonna tell me or not?"

"Sam is asking you to talk to the rudest person alive, he still comes after your father though." He spoke

"I thought you told me my father was just quiet and not rude."

"Well, I couldn't have acted like a fool and said that about your father like Sam did on the very first day we met...."

"HEY! I am not a fool"

"If you didn't know, yes you are"

"So, what was I saying? Yes!" and he continued. "But now I consider we are friends and I can tell you truth. Your father WAS rude. And so is the boy Sam is referring to and I don't think sharing the things with him you haven't even shared with your mother is gonna be a great idea. It's just murder of your confidence." Joe said and slammed his history book on the desk.

"He is saying that only because, he has had a few heated arguments with him and that for stupid reasons like he didn't apologize to me for calling me a nerd" Sam mimicked Joe.

"You are a NERD." Sam said again in a sarcastic tone.

"Yeah, yeah! Whatever."

"Anyway, what worse, getting your confidence or waking up to unwanted murder scenes and that in nightmares?" Sam asked throwing herself back to her seat.

"These kids sitting in the very first benches can leave the class to complete their important conversation." Sir Chadwik shouted from the lecture podium; his thin moustaches very parallel to the structure his eyebrows created.

She cleared her throat loud enough, so that the jet-black haired boy in front of her would be able to notice her.

"Sour throat?" He asked as he adjusted the books in his locker.

"Umm…. Sort of" She replied. They stared each other in awkwardness and then Savanna asked, "Are you Raf ebalore?"

"Hmmm"

"So…. did you…?"

"If in any case you want to talk to me. I am not interested." He asked and slammed the door of his lock

"Whao! What! Why would I…."

"So, it's you!" he said finally adjusting a second to look at her face.

"ME? what, you are confusing me."

"Just forget it." He stared at her eyes for another second before he added

"If you ever want to talk to me" he said and rummaged through his bag for a pen and a paper, wrote his number and gave it to her.

She accepted it but not accepting to ever use it.

"Was my information true then?" Sam asked.

"I don't know"

"How come you don't know? You were talking to him a minute ago. What were you talking about then?"

"I'd say joe was more right about him till now."

"Told yaa" Joe said.

"And how is he right?" Sam asked staring at him.

"So that Raf ebalore considered that I was interested in him. And God gracious rejected me."

"WHATT!??" Sam and Joe said together. Sam with surprise and joe with laughter.

"And gave me his number in case I needed him."

Both stared at her quietly.

"Sticking up with the plan of going to a psychiatrist sounds better. right?"

"Don't you think your left ear is a little smaller than other one?" Sam asked staring at one of the frames at her staircase wall.

In this one she was in the same winter sweater her father was wearing and both were laughing as the photographer captured the moment.

"Use your brain Sam, angle affects the photograph." Joe replied.

She took the frame out of the wall and stared examining it.

"Guys! I've got something to tell you." Sam walked to them with the frame in her hands and her super curly red hair untied.

"Another of your theory to prove my father a vampire?" Savanna asked.

"No… first I'll ask you a question."
"Okay, go on."
"When were you born?"
"16 years ago, of course."

"Year?"

"Use some basic calculations, Sam." Joe said.

"Wait a minute. I just need the answer from her mouth." She said not moving her eyes from the frame.

"2005. But why? What happened?"

"You sure?" Sam asked finally taking her eyes off the frame.

"Whoa! How can she not be sure about her own birth date?" Joe said as he turned from Sam to Savanna.

Savanna stared in silence when she heard Sam saying.

"Then, why does this frame say June 1986?"

Every photo frame had the years of early 90's. which could not possibly be true, Savanna wasn't even born back then.

"Do you think it's a kind of misprint or something else!" Joe asked searching at the back sides of the frame. He picked up from the piles they had collected from the wall and laid in front of them.

"Misprint in all these frames just doesn't make sense." Sam said

"What else should I be believing in?" Savanna asked Sam.

That night she decided to ask her grandmother about the wrong dates on the photo frames. She knew it wasn't a topic to be given such importance but what was wrong in asking? She searched for her grandmother in the verandah where she usually sat during nights.

"Don't you feel cold grandmother?"

"A little bit." She said as she noticed the unexpected arrival and shifted from her bench to make a seat for Savanna.

"But what you doing up so late." She continued.

"Teenagers nowadays stay awake often." Savanna replied declining the seat offered by her grandmother and rather sat on the floor between her grandmother's knees and gave her a bottle of coconut oil.

"My hair needs oiling."

"Don't you ever oil your hair?" Grandmother said as she lifted the bottle to squeeze out the oil.

"sometimes"

"Like? In a year?"

"May be"

"Sharin never knew how to be a mother; she has always been like a kid all her life"

"Anyway, how was it like?"

"What was what like?"

"My parents"

"What about them?" she asked and started massaging her scalp.

"What were they like? Did they like each other?"

"If they didn't, would I be oiling your hair right now?"

"Grandma! You are being............"

"Savage. As always" Grandma replied for her.

"Okay, all right. I'll better ask my mother about her relationship with my father."

"Then what will you do now?"

"Enjoy the massage"

"I've a better thing to offer"

"And what is it?"

"Would you like to listen a story?"

"Kids story?"

"Nop. A fairy tale"

"Don't you think, I am old for that now?"

"Fairy tales are not only for kids"

"Then for whom are they for? Adults?"

"Even old people."

"Seriously?"

"Do you even know what that means"

"I------"

"Do not even try. I don't want to hear any pathetic answers, I'll tell you by myself."

"Okay, go on."

"So that what my- grandmother told me fairy tales are, Ahmmm– so when children die at a young age. Their souls are automatically considered to be pure and innocent, not capable of committing any sin. Hence, they are directly sent to the fairies for one week, who live in a garden which lies between the earth and the heaven. They treat the children like their own assets and every night all the kids sit around the bonfire and share their death stories, almost all of them are normal natural deaths while a few are tragic and heart breaking.

Fairy's children also listen to these stories when the souls are sharing it. And as you know fairy's exchange their children with human children, and the fairies growing up in the human world grow up to be called the changelings.

Almost all of them do not remember that they are fairies and does not trigger any magical power, while some does, and those changelings in many legends gets evil. And the stories they share with the humans on the earth about the little children's deaths are known as fairy tales.

Chapter-4

THE MURDER

"I was born in a slum area, to the parents who already had three children before me and two after me. I never saw the youngest one's face though."

Granny squeezed the bottle to let the oil fall on her hair directly.

"I never went to school, didn't even knew there was anything like that until saw some kids in a similar uniform climbing into a yellow bus, then I didn't know what was that, until my elder brother told me." She replied and continued.

"My father worked as a wage labour and my mother as a maid, and it was never enough for the family. So, we were made to work in order to fill our stomachs. My sisters worked as my mother did, and my brothers and I collected plastics from slum. It was all going normal until one day a man with the same disability as I asked me if would like to have a chocolate, I never ate any in my whole life, I have only heard about it that it is delicious. Even though my mother used to tell me a hundred times not to take anything that a stranger offers, I accepted it. I haven't had any meal since last day, so I blindly accepted the chocolate. I was picking rag bottles from the slum that morning, when he arrived in his black car, as shown in the films. He had heavy moustache and a dashing personality but the same disability. I sat on the cars back seat tempted to drive it as he promised he would let me.

I was enjoying the car drive, looking out the window as the slums slid out of my sight, he gave me two more chocolates. I started to like him more than I did my parents, but then I suddenly felt sleepy and dozed off in the back seat. And when I woke up it was all dark around me, I couldn't figure out the objects the only light. I could see he was coming from the room behind the closed door above the stairs. I dozed off again a few seconds later, after realizing that my hands were tied at my back and I had a handkerchief stuffed in my mouth. Duct tape on it and on my ankles and then I was tied to a chair.

"The next time I woke up, I saw him standing in front of me with a rope in his hand. I panicked. I tried to shout, but my screams got muffled behind that cloth stuffed in my mouth. I thumped my feet with every inch of energy I had in me. As I was struggling, he started taking my life. It was the worst time I experienced in my life, not being able breath is more terrifying than anyone might expect. My body was tied to the chair. I couldn't let my arms and legs ask for freedom for life. Tears fell down my cheeks as my chest started to burn."

That murderer threw my body in a rag bag and dragged it out of the basement, out of the house. He threw me in a pit hole in the ground and covered it by soil and soil and more soil.

The last thing I remember is the other innocent soul looking at me with pity in their eyes from up above.

Chapter-5

I AM A VAMPIRE

"It isn't true? right?" Savanna asked.

"An innocent soul never lies" her grandmother replied as she tied her oily hair into a tight bun.

"Do you think this house is haunted!" Savanna asked her mother while she swiped Savanna's forehead with a hanky and the red from her head was cleaned off.

"No, and why would you think so?" Sharin asked back, chuckling at the question Savanna asked.

"May be because it's old enough to be home to at least a hundred ghosts.

"It seems to me like you have started listening to Sam more and Joe less." She replied unable to hide her smiling face. She tilted a cleanser bottle on a cotton ball and started taping it on her forehead gently.

"It hurts."

"It was the funniest way to get injured by the way" Sharin said and gave a full-fledged laugh.

Savanna was recording a video of balancing piles of books on both her hands, two on head and one between the teeth and carrying all these, she was jumping down the stairs on one leg. When on the fifth stair she accidently stepped on the step's edge resulting in her rolling down the stairs, hitting her arms, legs and lastly forehead on the edges.

"Whatever. I am still gonna get a treat from Sam." Savanna replied. Sam was the one who dared her to do that.

"I am sure now; you listen more to Sam than Joe."

Sharin walked past a photo frame of all three of them, the same one in the hall but in a larger frame, she placed the cleanser back into its place in the drawer.

"I would like to ask you something, even if you feel uncomfortable, awkward or if it hurts you." Savanna said.

"I'll be ready then."

"Why did you two get divorced?"

"Honestly" she took the most depressing sigh ever and continued.

"We didn't vibe anymore, I mean it was becoming difficult for both of us. We realized we loved each other but were not made for each other."

"So, you agree that you loved him?"

"Even now, darling."

"Then how come you never visited him all these years, not even calling him a complete cut off?"

"I-I wanted to never meet him because I thought I would never be able to get over him. I would have wanted to go back to him, being aware that we are never going to work out."

Saying this Sharin shifted on her bed to fold the blankets and Savanna caught a glance of a gold chain around her mother's neck.

Till now she had become habitual of the music playing in her room. It was so normal and regular now that she had figured out its time, that it would start playing at one in the morning and continue for half an hour while Savanna stuffed her ears with cotton trying to sleep or most of the time out of the room doing anything else but being in her room. As she had now developed a deep hatred for the music.

And this time she was again trying to sleep, her ears stuffed with cotton, lying on her bed, staring at the ceiling, trying her best to fall asleep. She stared at the ceiling, intricated with arche design and on the centre was.

"What is that" she murmured to herself, got up and dragged a chair to the center of the room placed another upon it and collected pillows, threw it on the pillar of chairs, she climbed on it and took a photo of the designs in the center, zoomed it, and noticed a disturbance in the wood, may be for a chandelier?

Or … may be.

She was still balancing herself on the chair pillar when she realized that the music was actually coming from the ceiling.

It was one hour now since the music stopped but she was still lying on her bed, thinking over and over. What was there in the attic? and why was it there? How could it still be working? And then she had to find it but how was she going to?

Her grandmother had cleared it out that all the door ways for the attic had been sealed for years now…. And would not be opened at any kind of request.

Busy in such thoughts of her she was startled when her phone rang. And was even more startled to see that it was Raf. She did save his number when he gave it to her just to make sure she wouldn't end up picking his call. But it didn't seem to be working when she felt an urge to pick his call.

"Hello" he said just as the call was picked.

"Hmmm…" she replied. Still not sure if he really meant to call her or it was a mistake.

"Am I talking to savanna?"

"Yesss. And would tell me why have you called?"

"So, you recognize me?"

"I saved your number. So, I'd knew whose call I wasn't supposed to pick?"

"Just because I rejected you?"

"First of everything I WAS NOT asking you out and the second I would be NEVER EVER be asking you out"

Savanna could swear he tried to hide his laugh.

"You sure about the second thing?" he asked teasingly

"So, you think I would?"

"May be"

"And now tell me quickly for whatever nonsense you have called me for I don't have much time to spend on you?"

"we'll see that" he whispered "well I was wondering if you'd be free someday. I mean" he coughed "maybe we could go out or something…"

"Whoa! Hold on. Who is the one asking now!?"

"Hey I am not asking you. Its just if you would like to spend some time nothing else."

It took her second to swallow down the whole situation and honestly, she wasn't even interested in finding his real motives she had something more important in her head.

"I'd go out with you…"

"that's great"

"I haven't finished. I would go out with you tonight only if…"

"What if it includes me jumping inside a volcano?"

"You'll have to do it then."

"ALRIGHT then. I promise I'll do it even if it includes me jumping inside a volcano."

"I am going to send you an address and you have to go there…."

"At this time of the night?"

"Or do you want me to not go out with you?"

"Dude that's blackmailing ………"

"Sounds nice like this."

He took a sigh full of regret and rage but continued.

"Hmm…. and what do I hear to do after that?"

"Then you would have to climb up to the roof. You can do that with the help of pipe lines."

"Whoo! Whoo! wait a minute. You want me to climb up someone's house at this point of time?"

"aren't you gonna do it then?"

"Go on" he sighed

"Then you would have to get to the roof and find if there is any portico there."

"You seriously think... I am gonna do that?"

"You seriously want me to tell everyone that you were not capable of doing a minor dare"

"Is this minor?"

"They wouldn't know it's major."

He stayed silent, maybe he was cursing the walls of his room. Until he spoke up.

"I am going to do that only because I am free tonight not because I am desperate for you or something. Got it?"

"Yes captain"

He sighed

"So, you are gonna do that?" She asked, surprised herself.

"Send me the address" saying this he hung up the call.

It was silent outside as the clock was ticking 11 of the night. Until she heard the noise of someone walking on metal stairs.

There were metal stairs in her house! She didn't know it. And the metal stairs were outside, not inside.

Because someone knocked the glass of her room's window. She was startled and ran to the window and drew the glass up from the sill.

He was standing there on a pipe.

"What the hell are you doing here?"

"Am I on the wrong address?"

"No, I mean what are you doing on my WINDOW." She said and looked out of that window to see the metal stairs, around 3 feet down.

"Oh…they, the stairs lead to the attic, I don't need to climb on the pipes anymore as you were advising me. but why did you suggest me that. You wanted me dead?"

"I didn't know, we had stairs here?"

"Wha….now don't you tell…. you don't know that your eyes…."

"No need. I know that" she replied immediately.

"You can join me yourself in this task of yours by the way. Your princess night suit wouldn't get ruined by climbing the metal stairs."

"Wow… am I supposed to jump down from here and not break my legs."

"Here is a pipeline, first step on it and then jump down"

"Don't you want to find a potico on your roof? But why would you want to find that? Just wondering." he asked.

"Because I need to get to the attic" she said and stepped out of her window.

"WHAT? You could have…"

"The doors are sealed, to the attic. portico can be the only door to go inside if any"

"Why are the doors sealed and why would you want to go there"

"You don't need to know" she said when he jumped down the pipe.

"I deserve to know. Its almost eleven in the night and I am here jumping at some random girl's window."

"That was your choice to do"

"Don't you know how to jump…....?" he asked as he noticed her hesitation to jump.

"As compared to you?" No, considering that you are an ancient ancestor of humans" she replied as she again stumbled upon the pipeline.

"Here put your foot on my shoulder." He said moving forward and placed his arms on the wall.

She did as he told and nearly fell on the stairs and tried to make the least noise she could, because the metal stairs were just as old as her house and they cried as if they were going to break down right now.

"What are you? A tonne?" he asked massaging his shoulders.

"And what are you? A stick?" she replied.

The stairs were straight and ascending to the top until she again had to climb a little to reach the roof and had to hear it again.

"One tonne three hundred and seventeen kilograms." Raf said helping her climb the roof

"Minus twelve kilograms." She replied

They walked to the spot, which she considered to be just at the top of her room.

"What is it there?" Raf asked.

"How would I know?"

"Pop your eyes out and see through the roof surface."

"How am I supposed to do that?"

"How would I know? This was your plan. So go on." "And it appears like there is no portico" he said moving his head to get a clearer look of the roof.

"Can you see these plates right there?" she pointed to her right side and laid down on the roof.

"Yup, these are solar panels." He said and sat next to her.

"And this is a good find I'd say"

"And now don't tell me that you didn't knew you had these solar panels on your roof?"

"No"

"God!" he exclaimed.

"No, I didn't know"

"Do you know ANYTHING about your home at all?"

"First thing this isn't my home and second, yes I do know something about this HOUSE and that is there are no electric appliances in our home, that work with solar energy."

"Then what are these solar panels doing at your roof? Belly dance?

"Exactly, it means they are still giving power to something."

"Any suspects then miss explorer?"

"No suspects. A clear criminal."

"What's it?"

"Do you think I am gonna share anything with you?"

"Ymmmm............ ok" he said.

"Until you promise you are not gonna blab it out."

"I promise and I don't break promises."

"I'd like to share something?"

"Go on"

"I experience nightmares quite frequently"

"Ohhh. I don't want to sound rude but I don't know how to react"

"And I don't want to say that but you sounded sweet for a second" she laughed.

"Oh thanks" he laughed back

"There is something that is triggering it, my nightmares by the way. and now the blurred images are like their pixels have been fixed, the noise is better and......they are getting more terrifying."

"And what's that?"

"The music, which plays every night in my room, it is somehow connected to the nightmares."

"How you guess these solar panels...."

"I am sure these solar panels give energy that musical instrument or whatever that is hidden in the attic, right above my head."

"Have you told anyone about?"

"About what?"

"That music."

"Yup."

"Who"

"Sam, Joe and you."

"I mean in your family"

"No one"

"And why so"

"My mom knows nothing about this house more than me, she isn't gonna help me if I tell her, she is going to only make me doubt my ears. and for my grandmother, what can she possibly do"

"So, what are you planning to do now?"

"Nothing. Just trying to convince my mom to let me sleep on the roof, the view is better here." She said gazing at the endless darkness and distant stars, which no doubt appeared to be heavenly more beautiful than in any encyclopedia.

"Seriously?"

"You stupid or something?"

"Okay, my bad."

"Why did you agree to help me even when what I asked from you was something ridiculous? Just curious" she asked

"Because………I have never had anyone ask me to do something for them. Everyone think of me to be rude. May be this is the first time I have helped anyone."

"And how does it feel to help a human for the first time" she asked chuckling.

"Great for sure, I hate humans by the way and this earth is full of them."

"I am vampire." she said feeling the goose bumps on her chin and the cold wind hitting her bare skin.

"Me too."

"Perfect."

Chapter-6
COUSIN

"I would like you to meet some of your relatives" Sharin said cleaning her hands off on her apron.

Their kitchen was messed up like it was never before and her grandmother was calm just as always.

"I have relatives?"

"From your father's side. Yes"

"They are from my dead sister's side of family and the only one we have, I guess." her grandmother said sipping her tea.

"And that was the last thing I could have ever expected" savanna said as she saw Raf giving sharin a box of sweets.

"You are my cousin?" she whispered in astonishment to him.

"Seems like asking you out wouldn't go out as I expected." He whispered back.

"You are really pretty" a woman with same jet black hair as Raf said this to savanna but more of her focus was on her eyes.

"Not all odd things are pretty" Raf said.

"HAHA funny" Savanna joked it off

That woman stared her son as if she was going to kill him the moment, they get home.

"I'd apologize for this behaviour of my son I just don't understand how does he manage to act in such manner every possible time" she gave her son a dead look before resting herself on the velvet sofas.

"Oh, its ok no one gets that"

"Gets what??"

"His idiotic behavior obviously"

"You know him already?"

"Yaaa, we are in the same school"

"Sounds nice" granny said over her tea.

They chatted the whole evening even though savanna found it quite exhausting, she did enjoy it. And it didn't much bother to her that Raf was her cousin. He although made jokes about it a time or two but he was cool about it too. They seemed to be nice people nothing rude like their son and even their son wasn't that rude like everyone else said. Sam might have been wrong about him.

Chapter-7

MUSIC BOX

"Does anyone of you have sickles at home?" savanna asked Sam and joe.

"My mother might have some but why?" Sam replied.

"Good then. Today I'll call you both and you will come to my house with the sickles. I've got an exciting thing for us to do

"If it doesn't include murdering someone them I'm in."

"Is he supposed to be here?"

"For your surprise he is sort of my friend now" savanna replied.

"We are friends?? I thought we were cousins." Raf whispered to her.

"Clench up your teeth and put your tongue on the upper part of your mouth" savanna whispered back.

"whatt !!!" he asked.

"SHUT UP!!" she said.

"And how come you guys become friends? I don't remember you both talking after he politely rejected you" joe asked.

"Ummmm well, since she asked me to perform a belly dance at the roof of her house" Raf said.

"On the roof? Woah !!!! what did you guys do ??" Sam asked.

"Belly dance sounds nice"

"Don't you think it would be nice to keep these talks for a better chit-chat moment and right now focus on the things we have for now"

"Like burying a dead body?" Sam asked.

"No actually for your disappointment, this isn't any murder documentary's shooting scene."

"So, my mother is out for tonight, and today is the best opportunity to break the walls of the attic"

"What? All of them said at the same time.

"Breaking down your house isn't as casual as you are saying it is" Joe reminded.

"And why would you even want to do that?" Raf asked.

"Don't you try to be that typical cousin" savanna snapped.

"You are trying to break this house down. Why shouldn't I be THAT TYPICAL cousin"

"Because this house isn't yours to break. AND you are my DISTANT cousin" she snapped back.

"You guys are cousins??" Joe and Sam asked almost together.

"Sounds nice. Doesn't it?" Savanna asked.

"Seems like you are not going to be together after all." Joe said.

"You look happy. Don't you?" Raf snapped.

"Why wouldn't I be? At least my best friend is not having a chance to end up with a guy who is probably not going to care about her" Joe snapped back

"I am your best friend??"

"WHOA! It's getting crazy here" Sam said widening her eyes at Savanna and giving her that 'you gotta do something' look.

"What is it?" Raf asked after what felt like decade. "Why do you hate me so much."

"It's not that I hate you. It's just... I KNOW you don't ACTUALLY like her"

"And who told you he LIKES me?" Savanna asked.

"No one important" Joe replied and stared dead at Raf for two seconds before he continued "My bad, I guess. Anyway, we should be getting back at, whatever ... umm savanna was saying" saying this he started rubbing his eyebrows.

"You know you've made it super awkward right?" Sam said.

"Hmmm I do. Just forget whatever happened and let's get back to whatever we were planning to. shouldn't we?"

"I'd prefer that too" savanna said "And ahhhh! Yes, the plan goes with Sam taking my grandmother out for a walk, keeping her away from here, meanwhile me, Joe and Raf would break the ceiling above the staircase that goes to the attic."

"If you are okay with that" savanna added after seeing them obviously not convinced faces"

"You were right Joe; I don't actually like her" Raf joked.

"Savanna why don't you come with us for a walk" her grandmother asked before stepping on the stone steps with Sam, who had an expression of 'I can't do it'

"No, I'm okay, moreover I've got to complete my assignment and Joe is helping me with it"

"Well, then you Raf? what about you?"

"Him? oh, he is a vampire, it is harmful for him to step out in the scorching sun. you know?" savanna answered for him.

"You didn't have to answer for me" Raf whispered to her.

"And you? Joe?"

"And him, he---has diarrhea"

"Oh! okay then, bye, have a good time" grandmother waved at them and left with Sam.

"Seriously? Diarrhea?" joe said meanwhile Raf was swallowing his laugh.

"You sure?" Raf asked handling a sickle in both his hands in an accurate angle to smash the ceiling in front of him. It was the third floor and they were standing in the confined abandoned stairs which were earlier to reach to the attic before it was closed. The ceiling to be broken were nothing but a sealed shaft of hard wood.

"Yes I am. for the fourth time"

"What if your mother abandons you for such an act of crime"

"You gonna do that or not?"

"For the last time......"

"Shut up!" she shouted.

And he smashed the sickle's metal head at the wood shaft, creating a crack at the centre, next Joe expanded the crack, they continued the work for a few minutes until the crack was a hole big enough for a human to slide through, and the first to slide through was savanna.

The attic was deserted and filthy. It was filled with cobwebs and spiders and a thick layer of dust everywhere. There was nothing in the whole attic except a machine in a corner attached with the wires to the roof.

"That it is" Savanna said.

It was an old music box, a big one though. Two inches of dust was resting on the cover it had. Making it questionable how was it working till now.

"And these wires must be connected to the solar panels above." Raf said pointing to the wires going all the way to the roof and vanishing there.

"Should we break it then?" Raf asked watching her caress that music box.

"Nope" she replied.

"Then why did you make us bang your roof? For nothing?"

"For surety"

"For what!"

"I wanted to make sure what exactly was here and that's all. Let's head back"

"HEY! You MUST see what I found" Joe shouted from another corner of the attic.

"What is it mate?"

"Mate? You guys already good?" Savanna asked kinda surprised at what she was seeing.

"Yaa boys aren't like girls, bitching and stuff. We say it straight and then we're good. Right dude?"

"Damn right" Raf replied and gave joe a high-five.

"And a few minutes ago, you guys were folding your sleeves back and ready to punch each other's faces." "Punch? I was ready to beat the shit out of him" Joe said.

"Ouch! It would have hurt yaa"

"Unbelievable" savanna murmured to herself

"Anyway, I am ought to suggest, savanna you should sell your house to film makers. God damnn it has got lots of interesting stuff" Joe said

"What?!"

"Have a look at what I found" Joe said and sat down and started to pull a wooden block away from the floor.

"Are we supposed to completely sabotage your house?" Raf asked savanna doubting what Joe was doing.

"I don't think we were—"

And just then the block came out and the folding stairs fell to a room. Her—

"it's my grand ma's room" she said not fully sure if she did belief in it herself.

"So, your grandmother visited the attic regularly to have a what CHIT-CHAT with that music box?" Sam asked expressing the disbelief savanna was having very perfectly.

"She surely doesn't know about it herself or planned not to close it or found it after the doorways to the attic were sealed because I can't imagine her climbing up there" Joe said.

That was making quiet much sense. Her old granny wasn't healthy enough to climb up the stairs and do—what? Nothing.

This topic was closed just after this. No time for things that doesn't deserve time.

"Is that you?" Raf asked pointing at the frame he was holding in his hands which he took out of the wall sideways to the staircase to the second floor. She was peeking out of window and that was of a treehouse.

"Yes, but I don't know where the photo was taken"

"You don't?"

"No"

"It's in your backyard you stupid. This treehouse"

"Here?"

"Whao! Raf knows more about your house than you do" Sam joked. "How do you know this?" savanna asked

"The day you asked to perform belly dance on your roof, remember? I kind didn't knew where your house's main door was not that I was going to ring the door bell. And I ended up at your backyard and there was this I am pretty sure the same treehouse.

Savanna never had been in this part of her house, the deep woods of her backyard. And here it was. Same as in the frame. But torn out.

"Everything related to this house is old" Savanna said

"And I' m pretty sure, so are you. Vampires are old anyways." Sam said.

"Vampires can bite too" Raf whispered to Sam before following Savanna to the trunk of the tree with a torch as it was pitch dark now that it was almost eight in the evening.

"What do you think you are gonna find out there" Joe asked.

Sam agreed and said," Ya! don't get your despair…..."

"Honestly, I don't know. HONESTLY, I don't know anything of what I am doing or what I am making you guys do with me. And HONESTLY, I have no idea WHY AM I DOING THIS. What am I trying to find?? A HIDDEN TRESURE FOR ME?? LEFT BY MY ANCESTORS?? OR A FAMILY SECRET?? LIKE SAM SAYS MY VAMPIRE BLOODLINE. AND I FOR GOD'S PLEASURE SHAN'T BE TRYING TO CONNECT ALL THIS WITH MY NIGHTMARES???"

"Dude you seriously think about those stupid vampire jokes I make. I was of course joking" Sam said barely aware of her voice after hearing an outburst of emotion savanna had.

"Youuuuu need to calm down" Raf said his eyes wide the same size Sam and Joe's were.

"Ya Ya, I do" she said and rubbed her temples. After a few seconds she stepped to climb up the stairs to the treehouse. And She was relieved to see that the door wasn't locked but wasn't relieved to see the shower of dust the moment she threw up the door.

"I've just discovered something" Raf said coughing heavily.

"Wott?"

"I'm allergic to dust"

"You'll be arachnophobic to the moment I tell you your messy black hair has a black spider relaxing on it"

"You are lying. Aren't you?"

"Not really" she replied and stepped on the wooden floor of the treehouse.

"There is no spider on my head, you were lying, and for your information, I am not ARACHNOPHOBIC"

He replied nothing to her, as she was busy staring a well-kept living room in front of her. The floor had no sign of dust. The couch looked as if it was cleaned a few hours before. The toys were kept in an arranged manner on the rack, sleek and clean.

"They aren't dusty." Raf said picking up a random toy from the shelf. "Seems like you've been playing with them for some time now" he chuckled. "Have you considered me to be like you?" she replied "These aren't mine.

"No, I haven't considered you to be like me. You are way rude then I ever was. And honestly its good these aren't yours. They appear to be creepy. All of them." He said picking up a doll.

And there was a juice can. On the table. With a date. A date! It didn't matter until she saw the date. A date. July, 1999. That was its manufacturing date. Almost 20 years old.

"Are you even listening to me?" Raf asked and placed the doll on the floor. Before savanna could have replied, the doll started moving on the floor and played the same music she couldn't bear anymore. She pressed both her ears tight to stop the noise of that music.

"Savanna, you, okay?"

She didn't reply. instead scratched the skin around her ears.

"STOP IT" she shouted and fell on the floor, head between her knees, eyes shut tight.

"What happened?" it was joe's voice, from the ground.

"I got it mate" Raf replied and ran to savanna "What is it" he sounded concerned but that wasn't savanna's concern at the moment all she thought about was to shut the music from reaching the skin of her ears.

"That music. Stop it RIGHT NOW"

It wasn't as if the music was hurting her but it was her hatred for it or better say it the fear of the music that she couldn't tolerate it any second more. Or maybe better call it the fear of the nightmares.

He ran back to the doll and tried to remove the key out of it in a hurry but it broke. Savanna might have started screaming if he wasn't in time to throw that doll out of the window, the music out of their reach. He slowly walked to her, sat beside her, and held her in his arms.

"It's okay. Its okay" he kept mumbling.

"It's the same"

"Same like what?" he kept his volume low

"Same like one in my room. The same one in my nightmares"

He fell quiet.

"It makes my nightmares more clear, scarier"

He didn't say anything, just held her tight and let her sob on his shoulder.

Chapter-8

REGIN'S DIARY

"The Meiji restoration." Joe said and took out a thin booklet from a shelf in Regin's office in Savanna's house.

"Mughals: friend or foe for the Indian culture" Savanna said picking up a heavy book from the pile she had spread on the floor.

Do you have any idea how much all these books cost?" He asked glancing over all the shelves and hundreds of books on them.

"Are you planning on selling them?

"In black market. Yes." He joked.

"We have found something really important" Sam shouted storming through the door with Raf.

"Let me guess, 10 years old peanut butter?" Joe asked.

"How can that possibly be important?" Raf asked entering the room just after Sam.

"The last time she found some in my grandparent's pantry, she considered it to be the greatest archeological artifact of all the time." Joe replied.

"I was a kid back then." Sam argued.

"A 13-year-old kid, YES." He said back

"Whatever, we've found something REAAALLY important." Sam continued.

"And it really is?"

"So, we were going through the stuff in the tree house. Raf and I. and we found a diary belonging back to 1999."

"Whoo! Everything in your life is related to the year 1999." Joe joked.

"And I wasn't even born then. Irony." Savanna said.

"Well maybe you were. We are vampires, aren't we? I myself was born in 1970." Raf said

"I knew it. At last, one of you confessed instead of joking about it" Sam said.

"Whose diary, is it?" Savanna asked ignoring Sam.

"We didn't check that, the moment I saw the year, one nine, nine and another nine. I just ran out of the treehouse nearly stumbling down, took no notice of Raf shouting behind me, just ran with the diary. I know very well how much obsessed my bestie is to that year. Actually, it didn't even matter to me that it was of that year I just brought it to you because it was a diary. Such kind of journals are important in movies and stuff and it was then I found it even more important when Raf told me about that juice can and I immediately connected it with those photoframe's date. And stuff" Sam said it almost three breaths and threw an old torn diary to her.

"would've been better handling that diary before you blabbed an entire speech" Joe said chuckling and sat down next to savanna to have a better look at that.

It was covered with brown leather scratched by rats at the corners and smelt like old sodden. And at its back over were some words scrabbed with some sharp instrument.

"I ended with you." Raf read

"What does that mean?" Savanna said back and opened the first page.

Year 1982 … and a dry piece of a huge petal taped under it.

"Do you think this flower is really that old?" Sam asked

"We can sell it at a good price at any antique shop." She continued.

BELONGS TO – REGIN SMITH

"So, this is my dad's diary?"

"Look at the last page, what's the date there?" Joe asked.

Savanna flipped through the pages and stopped on page no. 512 out of the total 700 pages book.

"June 17, 1999" Savanna read.

"Dear Kate" She continued.

"Who's Kate?" Raf asked.

"I am just as clueless as you are. She replied.

"My rafflesia" Joe read.

"Read the first diary entry." Joe suggested.

She flipped through the pages and stopped on the very first one.

"This it is" Sam said

Savanna placed the diary on the floor of the room and read out of it.

"Seventeen June, 1987."

"Waooooo this diary has seventeen years of vampire's life. This is gonna be epic." Sam said.

"Dear Kate"

"This is the most glorious day of my life. I ever had or even gonna have. You come into my life and this is where my life fully starts. I cannot express my love for you through any combination of twenty-six alphabets on a dead form of a tree. All this is extraordinary, beautiful, and amazing. I swear upon Saraswati, my goddess. You are gonna be the one, I am going to protect over my life, you are gonna be the one I am going to struggle any hardship through all my life."

"You'll be the one who is going to read this after I die. My everything is to you."

"Now I think I have an idea who Kate is?" Raf said.

"So does everyone in the room right?" Joe said.

"I was right the whole time." Sam said over exited.

"She is a vampire of course and she looks so young even when you are 36 years old."

"This isn't the time for jokes." Joe declared.

"Who the hell is Kate?" Savanna said frustrated out.

"Well, I'll suggest you only one thing. Read it in privacy. I know you haven't been close to your father but reading his diary might be overwhelming for you and as it looks like it contains secret, maybe it is personal then so...." Raf said

"Whoo! guys what if Kate is her mother's name?" Sam said

"I don't know." Savanna admitted.

Chapter-9

THE LULLABY

The music of the lullaby kept creeping in the background. And Savanna filled her ears with cotton balls and hid her head under mountain of pillows, all of the pillows she could find in her room. She didn't want to hear and then she wanted to hear. She wanted to face that music. The machine was old and rusted and wasn't creating perfect musical notes like the doll did. It wasn't rusted, but old, the doll's musical notes made it clear that the lullaby wasn't only some musical notes but it had lyrics, it had words. And she had to know what the words were. She couldn't bear to hear it herself closely it would make her go crazy. So, she asked Raf to sit in the attic and write down the lyrics for her. And she was here in her room, with clogged ears, trying her best to bear the music.

The moment music stopped she ran out of her, still maintaining her patience and climbed the stairs, whose wooden blocking they had together broken down. Raf was sitting just in front of the machine with a notepad.

"You got it?" she said and the sound echoed.

"And even matched the machine's lyrics with the doll's lyrics and guess what….? They are the same." He replied.

"So, what is it then? She whispered and walked up to them.

"My writing is bad though." He said and handed over the notepad.

"Read the first one, it's the same I heard from the doll now that I can't wind it again that's all I remember. Clear lyrics"

DOZE OFF... YOU LITTLE... IN SLEEP...

SNOOZE OFF...IN YOUR ... SWEET DREAMS...
DON'T YOU...FEAR THE DARK...
WE'LL PROTECT YOU FOREVER...
DON'T YOU FEAR... IT'S NOT GOING TO TEST ...
WE'LL BE WITH YOU FOREVER...
DOZE OFF... YOU LITTLE ... IN SLEEP ...
SNOOZE OFF...IN YOUR SWEET DREAMS...
DON'T BE AFRAID TO BE ALONE...
IF YOU FEAR THE MONSTERS
DON'T BE AFRAID. YOU'LL NEVER BE ALONE...
THEY ARENT DANGEROUS ...THESE MONSTERS...
DOZE OFF...YOU LITTLE...IN SLEEP...
SNOOZE OF...IN YOUR...SWEET DREAMS...

"Does this remind you anything? Raf asked.

"Nope. not even a little" she replied.

"Savanna, I-I need to tell you something" he said.

"Ya... go on" She replied still staring at the notepad.

"I need your full attention." He said a little serious this time.

She looked back at him when he said "Joe wasn't telling the truth when he said that I didn't ACTUALLY like you"

"I know that"

"He wasn't true about that I didn't ACTUALLY like you"
"Whattt?!"

"He is friends with one of my very close friend Evelyn who told him something that made him say that" he said and his fear easily visible on his face.

"What is it? What was that Evelyn said to Joe" savanna was getting interested.

"Evelyn told him that I liked you" he said and got very interested in his shoes.

"And why would she tell him that you like me?"

"ARE YOU DUMB?" he suddenly had no interest in his shoes.

"And how am I dumb?"

"Evelyn told Joe that I liked you because I LIKED YOU" he almost shouted the last sentence.

She stared right into his eyes in shock and somewhat horror.

"I still do" he sighed.

"But-no-it can't. How can you-we-I-mean-we're cousins."

She hadn't stopped mumbling till Raf kissed her. And she hadn't realized what happened not until he said.

"Ya we're cousins. Distant cousins and I am not saying it by myself. Your grandmother approved of it."

"Wait! What? You've already told my grandmother about it. Not-how-like-I mean-"

He kissed her again before she could've completed her sentence and this time he didn't part off after a second like before, neither did savanna hesitate.

"You like me?" he asked not believing in what he was asking

"SAVANNA!"

And that was it. All she needed for the beautiful moment, her beautiful mother.

"OUT OF EVERYONE IN THIS WORLD, YOU HAD TO CHOOSE HIM." Sharin shouted at Savanna, pacing around the living room trying her best to not rip out her hair.

"But I am ought to admit your daughter have a great choice." Grandmother said from her velvet sofa, chilling and sipping her tea with Raf sitting next to her, looking like he might throw up any second.

"Tell me Savanna, did you ever think that he is your cousin? Did you ever consider that if you two get serious--?"

"I am serious." Raf abruptly said and got away interested in his shoes when Savanna gave him a 'SHUT UP' look.

"TELL ME SHARIN, are they even cousins, does that matter?"

"How would you have felt if you had found me and Ragin snogging in your attic?"

"I don't want to lie but I kind of knew that you two definitely used to snog in his room."

"AT LEAST WE WEREN'T COUSINS." Sharin shouted; her face flicked red for a second.

"And, yes, it was really terrible to find your daughter snogging her cousin." Sharin continued trying to change the topic. "But that in the attic, how did you – I mean – that was closed, HOW DID YOU EVEN MANAGE TO BREAK THAT and why would you do that? I thought a thief or something might have barged in, and – then I found the Greatest – Surprise – Even"

"Back to shouting." Savanna whispered to Raf.

"And don't you do that whispering thing with that LOVER BOY of yours."

"My ears have started to hurt now, Raf, would you please grab me, my ear wax." Grandmother said to Raf in a low tone pointing to a drawer across the living room.

"Yeah, of course." He mumbled and did an awkward run to the drawer and grabbed the wax to run back as fast as he could.

"Savanna, this is not a request, this is an order. You must stop whatever is going between the both of you."

"What if I say, I won't." Savanna snapped back.

"So – you are saying you are going to choose him over me? Over your mother? And that temporary boy?"

"Why does he have to be a choice?'

"Because I don't want you with him. AND AS YOUR MOTHER I HAVE THE AUTHORITY TO STOP YOU FROM THAT."

"And why would you want to do that?"

"YOU – ARE – COUSINS AND COUSINS ARE NOT SUPPOSED TO BE SNOGGING EACH OTHER. DID YOU NOT EVEN FEEL A PERCENT OF SHAME DOING THAT? HOW COULD YOU LET HIM TOUCH YOU LIKE THAT?"

"KEEP HIM OUT OF THIS." Savanna snapped.

"LEAVE HIM." Sharin snapped back.

"Sharin, you shall not bring the kids into this." Grandmother said.

"What!" Savanna and Raf looked at her in astonishment.

"I know exactly why you don't want them to be together. And you shan't bring them into this. You shan't destroy their relation." She said her eyes almost filled with tears.

"Not bring us – into what?" Savanna asked moving her head to look at both of them.

"Sharin, I know your hatred for this house very well, I know that every second in this house is a year of severe pain to you. I know that you can't afford to be here more. It is already you. Moreover, even you, Savanna, you know, you two are going to stay here only until I die." Her voice cracked at this. "I don't know neither do I care or whether you are planning to sell this house after my death. But Sharin I know and I care that you shan't in good conscious destroy these kids – just because of your hatred."

The room fell silent and only the cracking of the fire could be heard. Sharin stared the grandmother with rage and tears in her eyes. She clinched her teeth so hard that it might start to pain. The silence remained until Sharin finally said looking not at Savanna but her grandmother.

"Leave him."

Grandmother adjusted her glasses and disappointment could be seen in her movement as she stood up slowly to leave the room.

"And you, Savanna, are going to leave him, because I don't want you to get heartbroken when I drag you out of this town the day your grandmother dies." Saying this Sharin left the living room wiping her eyes on her navy-blue sweater's sleeve.

"You should go now, Raf."

"You – tells me you are not really considering on leaving me."

"I am, actually."

"And why would you consider of doing that? He said in his squealing voice.

"My mother is right, isn't she? It was really disgusting of me. You are my cousin." She sighed.

"Distant." he added.

"But still cousins." She finished.

"Alright!" she stood up. "Leave me. It's okay. Just tell me for once you like me?" tears might have fallen from his eyes if he would have blinked.

"I don't." she completed and saw Raf bursting out of that Mahogany door and wishing that he didn't see her crossed fingers at her back.

It took Sam and Joe a complete minute to digest the scene of the attic and then an extra minute to digest the scene of the living room. And they stared her as if a highly prestigious medical institute declared her theory of two livers to be true.

"Well, Evelyn did tell me once that he liked you. And I thought that it might be a dare or something. They all play that stupid game." Joe completed.

"I guess, I liked you guys together." Sam said with a confused face.

"I didn't approve that guy for you from the very starting, and that not because I had some problem with him." He turned to Sam to say that, "That was only because I know that he was given a dare to call you and ask you out and that's what he was doing when you asked him to dance on that roof or whatever—"

"It was a dare?" Savanna asked.

'Didn't see, that coming." Sam said.

"Hmmmmm… that was. And that is why I never believed it when Evelyn told me that had started liking you, and I just never wanted him to be pranking on you or something. But I realized it that he liked you even before you would have realized."

"I did not, until he told me."

"But nothing about it matters now. Does it?"

It did not. Talking about him or thinking about him was more of a waste of time and energy, better call its wastage of emotions and that is when she took to hibernating in her room all day, bunking school as much as she could. Dozing off on that timing of music and directed herself towards her father's diary.

It took her almost fortnight to realize that fat diary had nothing but some poems, random drawings, and other useless stuff. And the things that might have been useful were all written in Sanskrit, a skill of her father she could boast about but did not like at all now as she could not read it anymore.

But she knew that her grandmother was the one who taught her father Sanskrit. She found it confusing whether she should ask for her help to translate the diary of her dead son. But what else could she be doing to distrait herself.

"Grandma!" she said knocking on her room's door.

No answer.

"Are you there? She asked again.

No answer.

The door was unlocked. She turned the knob and walked inside only to see the folding ladder hanging from the ceiling in front of her.

She waited there, waited for an explanation from her grandmother. She could hear the cracking of wood as her grandmother was reaching for the ladder. She saw her sitting down on her room's floor carpet and hesitated a second or two before climbing down of the ladder.

"What were you doing there?" Savanna asked just as her grandmother was done folding the stairs.

"Dusting." She replied not daring to look in to her face.

"Dusting …what? A music box?"

"I reckon you saw it, when you were there with Raf."

"I have been there before a lot."

"Might be when you broke the shaft?"

"Shouldn't you be answering ME NOW."

"I have to clean the box."

"And why do you have to?"

"If I don't, it wouldn't work."

"And why do you want it to work?"

"So that you would be able to listen to the music."

"And why would you want me to listen to that music?'

"I do not know; I do not know my child. That music box is lying there for years, now I must keep it going. I mean I have attachments with it. I cannot stop it."

"Is it somehow connected to me?"

"I – don't think so my child." She said with pity in her eyes.

"Then why does it – I mean – leave it anyway."

She didn't know if there really was something wrong or it was only her hallucination. She simply walked out of the room determined to never touch her father's diary again or ever wonder about her nightmares. If no one was going to give her answers nor she was going to ask.

Chapter-10
THE MURDERER

"Two and a half teaspoons of sugar" Sharin ordered.

"Check" Savanna replied and poured a teaspoon into the batter.

"Half teaspoon palm oil."

"Check" she said as she did so.

"Now mix the batter properly."

"Yes, caption." She replied and started mixing the dough batter.

"It's good enough now, put it in the oven."

Savanna did, as directed and set the oven on timer."

"Good job Savanna, if you keep practicing like this, no one's gonna abandon you as a wife in future." Sharin joked.

"Whoo! no one is ever gonna abandon me. I am amazing and gonna be an amazing wife."

"Umm..., planning of being a wife already, huh?" Sharin said and removed the apron she was wearing till now to reveal a pendant necklace on her chest.

"What's that?" Savanna asked utterly bemused.

The stone was emerald green and there was nothing special about it, nothing beautiful… it was only a normal pendant.

"It's a … pendant.' Sharin replied confused.

"Why is it not looking good one me?" she denied

"No, it's nice, but where did you get it from?"

She said trying to deny the odious theory popping in her head.

"I .... umm...... your father had gifted it to me on our anniversary, exactly eighteen years ago.' Sharin replied not sure of the dead expression of Savanna's face.

"Exactly?"

"Yes, It's our anniversary today." She hesitated.

"But why, Is there anything my dear? You look........."

"Revested..." Savanna completed for her.

Sharin didn't say anything further. It was clear on her face that she didn't understand a thing about what mood swing Savanna experienced that she was on a verge to burst out with tears. To not make the situation worse Sharin kept quiet and glanced at Savanna's teary eyes.

Savanna stepped back and storned out of the kitchen, out of the house, she didn't feel safe there anymore. She didn't know where she was going without her phone. She couldn't contact Sam or Joe and their houses were way too far away to walk to. Left with only option she made her mind and ran with her feet to Raf's house. It was nearest of any of her friends.

All the time she could think of nothing of but the terrible reality she had just discovered. The odious truth her mind could not digest. The odious truth she didn't want to accept. And now she didn't know how was she going to tell this to Raf., Sam or Joe. How was she going to tell them that the nightmare which haunted her for years aren't only nightmares. It is the truth she experienced when she was a helpless kid.

She was a victim of an odious crime. She didn't want to agree her own birth giver attempted to suck the soul out of that child, at her own child.

But why?

She didn't know what was she supposed to do now, and whom she was supposed to trust in.

But she knew one thing for very surely that the green stone on her mother's chest today was the same that the murderer wore in her nightmare.

Chapter-11

I WANTED A BETTER ENDING

Her mouth went dry but eyes were wet the moment she saw Raf.

"You……. Okey?" he asked as he noticed her devastated situation.

"I am not" she replied letting her tears fall down.

"It seems like something terrible has happened." He said and gestured her to walk inside.

She walked directly to the bean bag and crunched herself into a ball on it.

"What is it?" he asked casually pouring hot coffee from his thermal into a cup and passed it to Savanna.

She accepted it gently but didn't dare to sip any of it.

"Humm?"

She said nothing but stares in his brown eyes and shed tears.

"I know it's not about me, you don't like me to cry for me. what is it now. Tell me." She looked at him realizing she could never understand the way she did hurt him.

"I…… don't know how to explain it to you." She said and more tears fell down her checks.

"You want some biscuits?" he asked and smeared the tears from her checks.

"Do you think it's time for biscuits?" she asked wondering what in the world made him ask her for biscuits. she didn't have a chubby face like Sam to look funny even when crying.

"I only wanted to lighten the mood."

"Your mum isn't at home, right?" she asked finally sipping her coffee.

"Hmm… If she was here. She wouldn't have left me talk to you."

She looked at him questioningly so he replied.

"The day you cut it off completely with me. I came home and she saw me crying……"

"You were crying?"

"What else did you expect?"

"I ………"

"Oh oke…. I know you didn't think of me to be crying over you. Whatever, so she saw me crying that night on the same bean bag where you are sitting right now. And, she asked me about that. I think it took me about an hour to explain her about everything. And then she took to hating you."

"She doesn't like me?"

"Not anymore."

She nodded

"So, what is it? You are here for. I don't want to sound rude but both of us know you are not here to just-TALK."

She took a deep breath, before she could answer and then said.

"Those nightmares, they are real."

"They probably are" Raf admitted.

"And the girl in that, is me"

He didn't reply and Savanna didn't dare look at him.

"And that locket. Of the murderer." she chocked at this

"It belongs to my mother."

Chapter-12

OLD SOUL

She fell in sleep crying that day on that bean bag. She spent the whole day there, ignored her mother's messages and calls, not sure what she was going to do buy pretty sure that she wasn't going home. Raf gave her blankets which she smeared with her tears. And when she woke up in the morning, Raf offered her a cup of coffee.

"It's dark." he said.

"I'll need it." She said and accepted it.

"Actually, I didn't mean the coffee."

"Then what?"

"Whatever you told me about that nightmare of yours."

She nodded. "It is"

She spent the next week switching her residence from Sam's house to Joe's giving an excuse that they were working on some important school project. she couldn't go to Raf's of course his mother wouldn't let her in any way. She wasn't in enough strength to go to her home. She didn't let her mother meet her. Only what she did was shout at her mother for being a murderer two days after she ran away on a phone call.

And after that, her mother didn't try to contact back.

I had been two weeks but she couldn't dare go back to that so called 'home' filled with those so called 'family'.

"And here is where the story begins." Raf said as he slammed a novel on the table in their school library.

"What?" Savanna asked startled.

"I have just completed the first book of this series, you know what." He leaned closer to her.

"It's just the beginning."

And now Raf was talking to her, saying that they could keep it to being just friends. And it was working very well.

"I still don't understand how you guys manage to read books." Sam said flipping through a fat book, crouched on the chair as if it was a couch.

"It is not managing to read books. It is managing others things to read books." Joe said finally bringing his nose out of his book.

"By the way I have got to issue this one." He replied.

"I have one too." Savanna replied and grabbed a book from the shelf.

Both of them walked to the reception. The little deaf librarian nodded as Joe gestured him that they wanted to issue some books.

"How is it going with your mother?" Joe asked.

"I don't want to see her face." She snapped.

"Do you seriously think that there is any connection with that locket and your nightmare?" he said.

"You think there is not?" she snapped back.

"Just think over it, why would any mother try to kill their own child. The only family she was left with. You were everything to her, how could she ever try to hurt you, it's just a bunch of coincidences that you are thinking to be real."

"Even I don't want to hate her but what am I left with? Everything points at her. I can't live with someone I know is responsible for years of my distress. And she knew about my nightmares, she knew it and that is why she never took me to a doctor, I never told her the details like that pendant and that is why she ended up wearing in front of me not knowing I would notice."

"We are both bookaholics, aren't we?"

"And now you are trying to change the topic."

"Just trust the process, so, you a bookworm?"

"Hmm...."

"Well, once I was reading my book, just like always my grandfather wanted to spend some time with me and I was trying to ignore him was hella busy in reading that science stuff. That day my mother told me something, that might help you."

"Hmm. I am listening?"

"Not everything can be found in books or internet. These old souls, either pure or not, carry much more secrets and experiences any of your book can have."

"What are you exactly suggesting me to do?"

"I am referring to that old soul that loves you, she is the only one who would have the truth to this. And if she doesn't, no one does."

Chapter-13

IS IT TRUE?

She loved autumn but today, it felt rebellious. As the orange dry leaves fell on the ground, she wanted them to go back and attach to the branch, she right now hated the dry and cold winds brushing her hairs rough.

Maybe it felt so revolting because she was walking to the home she didn't want to visit.

The stone steps weren't aesthetic any more, not even the detailed mahogany door, nothing was beautiful anymore.

She rang the bell, she didn't know but she had an urge to ring the bell, it didn't feel like home anymore to enter without announcing.

Sharin opened the door her eyes were red already. As if she had been crying for an hour now. She hugged her, Savanna didn't resist, neither did she join. But it still didn't feel awkward and when she let go, Sharin was in tears.

"I need to see grandma." Sharin looked a little surprised but nodded for good and stepped aside to let Savanna in.

Savanna knew exactly where she had to go. To the veranda as always, it was evening time and her grandmother just like always was surely sitting there, knitting her next project and enjoying the oak tree dropping its leaves.

"So, how was it?" her grandmother said just the moment she stepped her foot on the veranda.

"What?"

"The sweater I sent you last week, I had been working on it for the last season and you weren't here when I completed, so I had to parcel it to Sam's address. By the way liqueur Prices nowadays are way too high then they ever were in my time."

"You used to drink?" Savanna asked surprised at what she had just heard.

"Then? What have you considered me to be, innocent like you? Sam told me the prices and I was taken a back for a moment."

"When did you guys talk about this. Urghhh, unbelievable."

"Well, this wasn't the answer to my question. How was the sweater?"

"Ummm... yeh, it was good. Warm, soft...."

"But uncomfortable."

"What? No"

"Yes, you have got rashes on your neck, see. Or either it's something you don't want to tell me but I'll still warn you. Your mother hasn't changed her decision about him."

"Granny! it's nothing like that, shut up."

"Humm.... hummm..., kids these days." Grandmother chuckled.

"You are teasing me."

"Yes, I am. and woah your hair are so rough let me oil them, bring some coconut oil and make sure to heat it otherwise it's only a piece of smashed and frozen coconut, and a glass of water too I am feeling thirsty."

Savanna set between her grandmother's knees and she poured hot oil on her head.

"This time it's not going to be fairy tales." Grandmother said.

"I know."

"Your mother understood everything the moment you accused her of being a murderer." She took a deep sigh before she continued.

And that moment I knew there is no point of hiding the secret from you."

"It's true then, she wanted to kill me?" she said barely able to digest it.

"No"

Chapter-14

NO LIES THIS TIME

"Your mother loves you and can never think of hurting you, EVER."

"Then, I must be sick. hallucinating things for years."

"No, my child no, you are not hallucinating, it's true, the nightmares are true, the incident was real. You are a survivor."

"Someone did try to murder me?"

"Hmmm, but it wasn't your mother, NEVER."

"Who was it then?" she swallowed ready for the answer knowing well enough the answer could not be worse than it being her mother.

"It was Regin Smith, your father." She said with great difficulty her voice trembling.

And that was it, she had enough material now to go crazy for. It was way too much her heart could bear.

She never knew him, but respected him, there was no hate in her mind for him, NEVER. She never met him but yes, he was her father. And how could he be her father....

"SHUT IT." She cried, stood up and ran away from her grandmother tears falling down her cheek faster than oil dripping down her forehead.

"SHUT IT" she shouted, "IT'S ENOUGH, I AM DONE WITH ALL THIS. All THESE LIES."

"This time, there are no lies." Her Grandmother promised her and for the first time she saw her eyes filled with tears. "Sit down my child." She said and gave her the glass of water.

"Fill your mouth full with water so you would keep quiet and let me complete the story. And remember if you step out of the veranda today, you are never going to find the truth anywhere else."

Savanna sat in front of her and did as she told her. Only wanting to know the truth.

"What were you told by your mother? That your parents were married in 2001? Right?"

Savanna nodded.

"They were married in 1981, at the age of 18 and 20."

Savanna wanted to swallow but knowing very well she had no questions to ask she let the water remain in her mouth.

"And the next year they had a daughter."

Savanna waited for more. She couldn't figure it out she didn't want to work her brain on it.

"You were born in 2005"

"So, the girl wasn't me." Savanna swallowed and said, and then again filled her mouth.

"They adored her, and Regin was like crazy over her, like really craz. He bought her everything she laid her eyes on. Things weren't going well between him and Sharin, so they both decided to take divorce, and willingly decided for their daughter to live with Regin. She was named Kate. Nothing much changed even after their divorce. Kate was happy with Regin and me, Sharin also visited often, he took great care of her being a single father. They got divorced in the year 1987."

"I used to love clicking pictures of them."

And hanging them on the walls." Said Savanna swallowing and filling her mouth with water again.

"Yes, those frames on the wall near the staircase are of Regin and Kate. I am sorry you were made to think that those were your photographs."

"It explains the dates on them." She completed.

"And if you ever noticed that Kate's left ear was a little different than the other in one of those black white frames."

"I-yeah. Sam did."

"She is an observer. When Kate was 4, she fell from the window of her treehouse and hit her left ear on the ground, she was hurt and the upper part of her ear was to be cut."

Savanna stayed quiet. her mouth filled with water. Not daring to ask or think any question. Just trying to let those things dissolve in her mind and trying her best to not let her sanity go.

"Everything was great until the calendar fell to the autumn of the year 1999."

"The worse year that could have been lived by my son. The year when Kate left us."

Her Grandmother let out a cry, not being capable of holding back her tears.

"Your father was devasted his miserable condition can never be described in words. The first year after Kate left us is just a blur. I don't remember anything and the next was full of Regin's madness."

"I don't know how to say this but to begin with the first thing he did was breaking all the mirrors in the house he even dismantled a pond at the backyard of our home."

Savanna looked at her with tears in her eyes.

"Come here." She took out a pocket mirror from her basket's pocket and showed it to Savanna.

This is the only mirror we have in this house; your grandfather had gifted it to me." she looked at her wrinkled face for a second before lifting it to Savanna. She wondered how many secrets she kept hidden behind those wrinkles of her.

"Look at your face." She did, it was pathetic.

"Now look at your eyes."

Her eyes. These eyes. Everyone would notice. One brown and the other green.

"Regin had the same, and so did Kate. He knew to get over her was to forget her, but every time he looked at himself in the mirror, he would always get a glimpse of Kate. And that is why he smashed all the mirrors in this house. And the next thing he did was to slaughter our neighbor's Siberian husky, it had heterochromia, just as you, Regin and Kate. And Regin could never bear someone like Kate being alive, he thought-if Kate isn't alive then no one gets to have their life, and your father stole that husky and killed it. Buried the body under the pine's tree in the backyard."

Savanna knew very well whose husky she was talking about.

"And the next thing I am going to tell you." She took a deep sobbing breath. "Makes me feel disgusted for being his mother. But I don't need to tell you. I have already told you about this."

"When?"

"Remember the fairytale I told you about the slum kid?"

"It-can't be." Savanna gasped trying her best to not throw up.

"Me too, I too never wanted it to be true, but it is, I could never have accepted it but he told it to me himself, as if he was a child and won in a race. I knew that day I was losing him." It could be seen how hard she was trying to keep on going with the story, her voice was making it impossible for her to keep talking.

"Sharin was back to help him get out of the trauma. And I remember how she used to cry to me about not being able to make him better."

"The night he buried the boy's body under the pine tree. He gifted your mother a locket. Yes, the same locket, and have a look at this page I found in your mother's diary, she wrote in diaries for a while when she was going through all this, she thought that it might help her, help her go through all of that, that's kind of a legacy in our family to write diaries, I do, Regin and Kate did, and sharin tried." She said and handed her a page she took out of her pocket.

"I was cleaning my dressing table (without a mirror) that evening when he came to me and slid an emerald locket down on my neck and whispered

'I love you'."

"I was overjoyed to hear it after years but before I could reply, he said.

But I loved her too. And broke down on my neck."

"I know he is going through a lot but am I not? What does he think, only he loved her? I loved her too!"

"But the time his activities reached its peak was when he tried to." She took a deep breath. "Take your life." You were only five then.

"Your mother was lucky to get in time, she was protecting you from him, not hurt you. You might have seen her pendent when she was dragging him out of there and you considered it to be the murderer's." she swallowed and closed her eyes letting the tears fall down her cheeks and took few seconds to continue.

"Kate was afraid of dark, she thought that the monsters of the dark would drag her with them to their kingdom." She said and traced her finger under her eyes. Clearing off a tear drop.

"Sharin wrote a lullaby for her and used to sing it for her before sleeping. But when they were getting divorced, she recorded her voice in a music box and placed it on the attic and connected it with the solar panels just so that it would play during the nights and Kate would sleep peacefully."

"So, that was Kate's room?"

"It was, and it was the same room where Regin tried to kill you at the same time when the music was playing, and that might be why this music revives your memories of that incident."

"We knew it all along what the nightmares were, just couldn't tell you the truth, you were so young. I would not have been telling you all this now too. But you couldn't be kept in dark anymore."

"Is there any dark left now." She said taking the hardest swallow.

"The most horrifying one is left."

"Your father was losing his sanity. And we tried our best to bring it back, to bring him back, but it was all in vain, he was not getting better and that is when your mother decided to bring someone else help him."

"What do you mean?" Savanna gasped trying to stop the theory popping in her head.

"She thought that may be someone who was like Kate would help him move on, she can do that."

"She could do what?" Savanna said.

"Sharin asked the adoption centers for a baby girl with a condition of heterochromia." Her grandmother completed.

"You mean that........"

"Yes, I am saying that you are-adopted my child."

Chapter-15

THESE EYES

Savanna ran down the staircase to her mother, who was sitting on the sofa, she hugged her not letting her go.

"I love you, Mom." It felt grateful to be calling her mom.

"I love you too." She replied and this time the hug did feel like a hug.

She walked out of the house and now it was dark.

She knew whom she wanted to spend her last hours of this terrible autumn day with. She called Raf and he had to lie to his mother to go out with her.

She waited for him outside and he was there in a few minutes.

"It wasn't my mother." She said before he could stop gasping for breath.

"Of course, she wasn't! we knew it. It was just your hallucinations."

"Yep, they were." She lied, deciding to never tell the truth to him or Sam or Joe. "Turns out you guys were right this whole time. Mum says these are because of a haunted T.V. show I used to watch when I was a child."

"All this for nothing?" he joked.

"Yes, all this for nothing." She agreed.

"I was wondering if we could just, like before-sit at the roof of my house and talk for some time."

"Isn't it cold?" He asked helping her climb up to the roof.

"Is it?"

"Yes, of course it is."

"Take my overcoat then." She said and handed him her long brown overcoat.

"What are you? A vampire...? don't you feel cold?" he joked.

"If Sam was here, she would have declared me one for sure."

"Ya, for sure." He laughed.

She wasn't in any energy to laugh but was pretty sure the only way to feel better was spend some time with her friends, and consider these nightmares of her, just hallucinations of her mind. Just like friends her friends. And this terrible autumn day, another nightmare.

Everything is to be lost one day, nothing stays forever. She would even eventually lose everyone in her life, but not now. But what matters is the moment. doesn't matter if it isn't a forever kind of thing but the joy and the happiness felt, stays in the moment. FOREVER.

She didn't know if it was Raf with whom she was Going to share her life, maybe it would be someone else as her life takes her, but it doesn't mean he would be nothing for her, this was the moment and it was enough.

Nothing could change the fact that wherever she belonged to, but where ever she was now, was enough and beautiful. The end is never the beauty, the journey is. And her journey with her mother and her grandmother was going to be beautiful.

"What are you staring it?" Raf asked blushing hard.

"These Eyes" she said with a smile.

"My eyes aren't beautiful, it's your eyes that's beautiful, my Husky."

www.ingramcontent.com/pod-product-compliance
Lightning Source LLC
La Vergne TN
LVHW091617170726
843492LV00007B/2462